Lisa D. Hoff

# SANTA FE

## NEW MEXICO

Self-guided Tours in 88 Pictures

# SANTA FE — PAST AND PRESENT

In the summer of 1598, a long train of wagons, pack animals, horses, cattle, sheep, goats, 129 soldier-settlers, their families, Indian servants, and eight Franciscan friars arrived at the upper Rio Grande to build the first permanent Spanish colony in New Mexico.

The first two settlements were not successful and, finally, decimated by starvation, desertion and Indian revolts, they were abandoned in favor of a new beginning on the banks of the Santa Fe River.

It was the second governor of the province, Don Pedro de Peralta, who established La Villa Real de Santa Fe (the Royal City of the Holy Faith) as the capital of Nuevo Mejico in 1610 under orders from Philip III of Spain.

Life remained precarious and rough for the colonists in the new location, but they gradually began to adapt to the environment, and giving up their dream of finding the legendary "Cities of Gold," they settled down to colonize the new province. Each family received two lots for a house and a garden, two neighboring fields to grow vegetables, two additional fields for growing vineyards and olives, and about 133 acres of land. In return for their land and water rights, settlers were obliged to live in the city for 10 consecutive years, to grow crops on their lands, to help maintain the "acequias" (irrigation canals), and to stand ready to serve as unpaid soldiers when necessary. Throughout the early 1600's, the colonial population of Santa Fe held steady at about 250 farmers, artisans, traders, missionaries and other frontiersmen, and 750 Indian servants. The settlers lived in flat adobe houses outside the enclosed plaza; the Indian servants lived in their own neighborhood across the Santa Fe River. The Plaza with its government houses (Casas Reales) at one end, and adobe church at the other, was the civil and spiritual center of the capital.

Although the King in Spain, the Viceroy in Mexico, and the Laws of the Indies, clearly intended to protect the Indians from abuse at the hands of the governors and settlers, they suffered under the sovereignty of the Spaniards. The Indians had to work for the settlers and the missionaries for little or no pay, they were often forbidden to practice their religions or live according to their traditions, and they had to pay tribute in corn, hides and blankets to the governor and to those settlers who had received a trusteeship over Indians as payment for their services to Spain. Indian resentment erupted in the Pueblo Revolt of 1680. The uprising ended with the Spaniards abandoning Santa Fe and New Mexico and retreating to El Paso, where they remained for the next 12 years.

In 1692, Diego de Vargas, the newly appointed governor of New Mexico, recaptured the city, and the following year, the settlers returned and started rebuilding Santa Fe.

The 1700's in Santa Fe saw only a few changes from the preceding century. People still bartered with chiles, corn, peas, sheep and other products and animals in exchange for services, goods and even lands - money was not introduced until the end of the century. The governor continued to quarrel with the friars and the cabildo (government), and Santa Feans kept on enjoying themselves at fiestas, fandangos (dances), and in gambling houses. They went to cock fights, to parades, watched the Indian dances in the Plaza or the dramatic presentations of historical and Biblical themes. The furnishings and decorations in homes were simple, and mostly made locally. Meals were cooked in the fireplace in heavy kettles or outside in "hornos," beehive-shaped adobe ovens, and were served on pottery made by the Pueblos.

After the Pueblo Revolt, the lives of the Indians improved somewhat, although the governors, the political officials in charge of the pueblos, and wealthy landowners still extracted harsh fees and fines in the form of produce and labor from them, but at least the government stopped to try to integrate them into Spanish society, and the church ignored the practice of pre-Christian rituals and ceremonies.

In 1821, a momentous change took place in Mexico which was to influence the future of all Spanish possessions in America. Mexico gained its independence from Spain. Gradually life in New Mexico began to change. With the new Mexican constitution came citizenship for Indians, free trade and free speech, the abolishment of the old Spanish caste system, and something New Mexicans had managed to circumvent for over 200 years: direct taxation.

In 1821, a trader from Franklin, Missouri, William Becknell, set out along old Indian trails and along the tracks made by mountain men with a string of pack mules loaded with dry goods. He arrived in Santa Fe three months later to the cheers of all Santa Fe who were eagerly waiting in the Plaza to buy his goods. In the years that followed, the trail to New Mexico became a major international thoroughfare. It was not long, however, before the Santa Fe market was saturated with goods, and soon some of the traders directed their freight wagons down the old Camino Real to Chihuahua City. Since each trader had to stop at the customs house in Santa Fe to pay duties on their freight, the city became the prosperous center of a lively trade in both directions. Some caravans had as many as 636 wagons, engaged 750 teamsters and drovers, and carried goods worth one million dollars. When they returned to Missouri they were loaded with Mexican silver bullions, furs, blankets and sheep fleeces.

In 1846, Congress declared war on Mexico in order to clarify their long dispute over the boundary line between Texas and Mexico, and the status of Texas, which had been admitted to the Union in 1845, even though Mexico still considered it one of their districts. A few months later, Colonel Kearny led his Army of the West into the Plaza of Santa Fe and claimed Santa Fe and New Mexico for the United States.

Changes came quickly: the first American newspaper in English and Spanish was founded, regular mail service from Missouri to New Mexico was established, a stagecoach crossed the plains once a month, and the volume and value of goods shipped on the Santa Fe Trail tripled. A new archbishop instigated the opening of a hospital, an orphanage and schools. Even the look of Santa Fe changed as it adopted white picket fences, gabled houses, flower gardens and walkways. New ordinances prohibited the camping of the wagon trains on the Plaza, butchers could no longer slaughter on the Plaza, nor drunken men sleep there. Santa Fe was becoming civilized.

Meanwhile, the Hispanic and the Indian population felt threatened as more and more Anglo-American settlers ignored Spanish land grants and their rights to their ancestral lands. There were increased attacks on settlers by Indians and attempts at insurrection by Hispanic New Mexicans. When, in 1880, the first engine steamed into Santa Fe, followed by demands for cattle and sheep, the Indian- and Spanish-Americans lost the lands that had been theirs for centuries to land speculators and cattle companies.

New Mexico became the 47th state on January 6, 1912. During the 1920's, New Mexico's heritage, its beautiful scenery and unusual colors attracted artists from all over the United States, who in turn gave the American public fascinating descriptions of the landscape, architecture and arts and crafts of the Southwest.

Today, Santa Fe with its opera, concerts, museums, galleries, special shows, dances and theaters is recognized as one of the nation's cultural meccas.

# L'HISTOIRE DE SANTA FE.

L'été 1598, une longue caravane de charrettes, d'animaux de bât, de chevaux, de bétail, 129 soldats avec leurs familles et servants indiens, ainsi que huit Franciscains arrivèrent sur le haut du fleuve Rio Grande pour y construire une colonie espagnole permanente.

Les pionniers eurent de grandes difficultés à s'établir et, décimés par des révoltes indiennes et des désertions, abandonnèrent leur première colonie et recommencèrent au bord d'une petite rivière.

La Villa Real de Santa Fe (la Cité Royale de la Sainte Foi) fut établi sous l'ordre du roi d'Espagne, Philip III, comme capitale de la province du Nouveau-Mexique par le gouverneur Don Pedro de Peralta, en 1610.

La vie dans la nouvelle cité n'était pas facile, mais petit à petit les colonistes s'adaptèrent au climat et à l'arridité du terrain, et abandonnant leurs rêves de trouver les fabuleuses "Cités d'Or", commencèrent à coloniser la nouvelle province espagnole. Chaque famille reçut assez de terrain pour une maison et un jardin, et 54 hectares de champs pour y cultiver de la vigne et des oliviers. En échange, les colonisateurs étaient obligés de vivre dans la cité pour dix ans, de cultiver leurs champs, de maintenir les fosses d'irrigation et d'être prêts à servir leur roi comme soldats. Au 17e siècle, la population de Santa Fe comptait 250 fermiers, artisans, commerçants, missionnaires et 750 servants indiens. Les petites maisons d'adobe des pionniers entouraient la Plaza fortifiée, tandis que les servants vivaient de l'autre côté de la rivière. La Plaza avec ses casas reales (l'administration) et son église était le centre civil et spirituel de la province.

Bien que le roi d'Espagne, le vice-roi du Mexique et les lois des Indes grantissaient la protection des indiens, ceux-ci souffrirent aux mains des Espagnols. Ils durent travailler pour les propriétaires fonciers et les missionnaires sans être payés, ne purent pas pratiquer leur religion ou vivre selon les traditions le leurs ancêtres, et durent donner des peaux, du maïs et des couvertures en tribut. En 1680, le ressentiment des indiens éclata dans la Révolte de Pueblo. Les Espagnols durent abandonner Santa Fe et le Nouveau-Mexique. Pendant douze ans, ils furent exilés à El Paso. En 1692, le nouveau gouverneur, Diego de Vargas, reprit la cité.

La vie de Santa Fe au 18e siècle ne changeait que peu. Les gens troquaient des piments, des moutons et d'autres produits contre des services, des marchandises et des terrains. Le gouverneur continuait ses disputes avec les Franciscains et le cabildo (gouvernement), les Santa Féans continuaient à se rejouir aux bals, aux fiestas et aux combats de coqs. Ils allaient à la Plaza voir des parades, des présentations de théâtre et des danses indiennes. Les meubles et les décorations des maisons étaient simples. On faisait la cuisine à feu ouvert ou dehors dans des "hornos", des fourneaux en forme de ruches.

Après la Révolte de Pueblo, la condition sociale des indiens s'améliora un peu. Bien que les gouverneurs, les propriétaires et les administrateurs des pueblos demandaient encore des tributs sous forme de produits agricoles et de travaux forcés, ils étaient libres de vivre selon leurs traditions et rituels religieux.

En 1821, un événement allait changer l'avenir de toutes les possessions espagnoles au nouvau monde. Le Mexique gagna son indépendance de l'Espagne. Petit à petit la vie au Nouveau-Mexique commença à changer. La nouvelle constitution mexicaine accorda la citoyenneté aux indiens, libéra le commerce, garantit la liberté d'expression et abolit les castes sociales instaurées par les Espagnols.

Encore en 1821, le marchand William Becknell partit de Franklin, Missouri, avec une caravane chargée d'articles de luxe. Il arriva au Nouveau-Mexique trois mois plus tard aux acclamations de tout Santa Fe. Dans les années suivantes la route à travers les plaines d'Amérique devint une route importante du commerce international. Bientôt le marché de Santa Fe fut saturé et les commerçants continuèrent avec leurs caravanes sur l'ancien Camino Real jusqu'à Chihuahua City au Mexique. Santa Fe devint le centre d'un commerce vivant. Quelques unes des caravanes avaient plus de 600 charrettes, avec 750 charretiers et guides, et amenaient des marchandises de plus d'un million de dollars. Du Mexique ils amenaient de l'argent en lingots, des fourrures et des toisons de moutons.

En 1846, le congrès américain déclara la guerre au Mexique pour régler la frontière entre le Texas et le Mexique, ainsi que le statut du Texas qu'il avait admis à l'Union en 1845. Quelques mois plus tard, le colonel Kearny et son Armée de l'Ouest, entrèrent dans la Plaza de Santa Fe en vainqueurs, et reclamèrent le Nouveau-Mexique pour les États-Unis.

La vie changea de nouveau. Un journal en anglais et espagnol informait les Santa Féans des événements politiques à Washington et à New York, un transport postal entre le Missouri et le Nouveau-Mexique les lia à l'est, et une fois par mois, la diligence amenait des visiteurs à travers la Prairie. La valeur des marchandises transportées par la route de Santa Fe se multiplia. Un nouvel archevêque vint de France et commença à construire un hôpital, un orphelinat et des écoles. Même la cité changea: des clôtures blanches, des maisons à pignons, des jardins de fleurs et des trottoirs longèrent les rues. Des ordonnances interdirent aux caravanes de camper sur la Plaza, aux bouchers d'y abattre les bestiaux et aux ivrognes d'y dormir. Santa Fe devint civilisée.

En attendant, dans la campagne, les indiens et les rancheros hispaniques durent se défendre contre les colonisateurs américains qui, ignorant leurs droits sur les terres, occupèrent des terrains qui avaient été les leurs depuis des centaines d'années. Quand en 1880, le chemin de fer joignit le Nouveau-Mexique à la côte atlantique de l'Amérique, ils perdirent leurs terrains aux spéculateurs et aux compagnies d'élevage.

Le 6 Janvier 1912, le Nouveau-Mexique devint le 47e état.

Pendant les années 1920, des artistes de tous les coins du monde arrivèrent au Nouveau-Mexique, attirés par son histoire, ses traditions, son paysage et ses couleurs. Ils fournirent au public des descriptions fascinantes du pays, des arts et métiers, et de l'architecture.

Aujourd'hui, Santa Fe avec son opéra, ses musées, ses ensembles de danse et de théâtre est une des centres culturels des États-Unis.

# DIE GESCHICHTE DER STADT SANTA FE.

Im Sommer des Jahres 1598 kam eine lange, schwerfällige Karawane, bestehend aus Wagen, Lasttieren, Pferden, Schafen, Rindern, acht Franziskaner Missionären und 129 Siedlern sowie deren Familien und indianische Diener an den Oberlauf des Rio Grande, um die erste spanische Kolonie in Neu Mexico zu errichten.

Die ersten Siedlungen waren nicht erfolgreich und wurden schließlich aufgegeben. Die durch Hunger, Desertation und Indianerrevolten stark dezimierten Siedler beschlossen etwas südlicher am Ufer des Santa Fe Flusses neu zu beginnen.

1610 legte Don Pedro de Peralta, der zweite Gouverneur der Provinz, den Grundstein für "la Villa Real de Santa Fe" (die königliche Stadt des heiligen Glaubens) und ernannte sie auf Befehl Phillips III., König von Spanien, zur Hauptstadt von Nuevo Mejico.

Das Leben in der neuen Hauptstadt war schwierig, jedoch lernten die Siedler sich dem harten Land anzupassen und konzentrierten sich, nachdem sie endlich den Traum, die legendären Städte aus Gold zu finden, aufgegeben hatten, darauf, die neue Provinz zu kolonisieren. Jede Familie erhielt zwei Parzellen Land für ein Haus und einen Garten, zwei Felder für Wein- und Olivenanbau und zusätzlich 330 Hektar Land. Als Gegenleistung mußten sie sich verpflichten, zehn Jahre in Santa Fe zu leben, das Land zu bebauen, die Bewässerungskanäle in gutem Stand zu halten und bereit zu sein, ihrem Gouverneur als Soldaten ohne Bezahlung zur Verfügung zu stehen. Während des 17. Jahrhunderts zählte die Bevölkerung Santa Fes 250 Bauern, Handwerker, Händler, Missionäre und andere Grenzansiedler, außerdem lebten noch 750 Diener auf der anderen Seite des Flusses. Die Siedler wohnten in flachen Adobehäusern rund um die Plaza, die das geistige und weltliche Zentrum der Stadt war.

Obwohl die Verordnungen des spanischen Königs und des Vizekönigs von Mexiko, wie auch die Gesetze der Kolonien versuchten, die Indianer vor Ausnützungen durch die Gouverneure und Siedler zu schützen, litten die Indianer sehr unter der Herrschaft der Spanier. Sie mußten schwere Fronarbeiten leisten, durften ihre religiösen Zeremonien nicht ausüben und mußten übertriebene Tribute an Mais, Häuten und Decken an den Gouverneur und einige privilegierte Siedler entrichten. 1680 war die Geduld der Indianer am Ende und sie lehnten sich gegen diese Ausbeutung auf. Die Pueblo Revolte endete mit der Flucht der Spanier nach El Paso, wo sie 12 Jahre lang im Exil lebten.

Im Jahre 1692 eroberte Diego de Vargas, neuernannter Gouverneur von Neu Mexico, die Stadt zurück und begann Santa Fe wiederaufzubauen.

Das 18. Jahrhundert brachte nur wenige Veränderungen. Die Einwohner tauschten immer noch Paprikaschoten, Getreide, Erbsen, Schafe und andere Produkte gegen Dienstleistungen, Konsumgüter und sogar Land ein – Geld wurde erst gegen Ende des Jahrhunderts eingeführt. Der Gouverneur stritt sich weiterhin mit den geistlichen Brüdern und dem "Cabildo" (Regierung), während die Santa Feaner das Leben bei Tänzen, Festen und in Spielhallen genossen. Sie verwetteten ihr Geld bei Hahnenkämpfen, sahen sich Festzüge, Indianertänze oder dramatische Theatervorführungen über geschichtliche und biblische Themen in der Plaza an. Die Häuser waren einfach eingerichtet und geschmückt. Die Möbel und der Zierat wurden meistens in der Umgebung hergestellt. Die Mahlzeiten wurden entweder in grossen Töpfen im offenen Kamin oder in "Hornos" vor dem Hause gekocht und in Pueblos-Keramikwaren serviert.

Nach dem Pueblo Aufstand verbesserten sich die Lebensbedingungen der Indianer etwas, obwohl sie immer noch riesige Abgaben an den Gouverneur, die Landbesitzer und an die Verwalter der Pueblos bezahlen mußten, aber zumindest gab die Regierung den Versuch, sie in die spanische Gesellschaft einzugliedern, auf, und die Kirche ignorierte ihre religiösen Zeremonien und Bräuche.

1821 trat etwas ein, was die Zukunft aller spanischen Besitzungen in Amerika ändern sollte: Mexiko wurde eine unabhängige Republik. Die neue mexikanische Verfassung brachte Handels- und Redefreiheit, die Abschaffung des spanischen Kastensystems, volle Staatsbürgerrechte für die Indianer und direkte Besteuerung.

William Becknell, ein Händler in Franklin, Missouri, machte sich 1821 mit einer Anzahl von Packeseln, beladen mit Kurzwaren und Luxusgütern, auf den Weg. Seine mühsame Reise durch zum Teil feindliches Indianergebiet endete drei Monate später, als er unter großem Hurra der Bevölkerung in der Plaza von Santa Fe ankam. In den folgenden Jahren wurde der Santa Fe Trail zu einem häufig benützten Durchzugsweg. Allerdings war der Santa Fe Markt bald erschöpft, und die Händler mußten sich nach neuen Absatzmärkten umsehen. Innerhalb kürzester Zeit plagten sich die schwerfälligen Züge auf dem alten Camino Real (königlichen Weg) nach Chihuahua City. Santa Fe, wo die Händler ihre Abgaben leisten mußten, wurde das wohlhabende Zentrum eines lebhaften Handels in beiden Richtungen. Manche Karawanen bestanden aus 636 Wagen mit 750 Fuhrmännern und Viehtreibern und beförderten Güter im Werte von einer Million Dollar. Auf dem Rückweg nach Missouri waren die Wagen mit mexikanischen Silberbarren, Fellen, Häuten und Schafsfellen beladen.

1846 erklärte der amerikanische Kongreß Mexiko den Krieg, damit endlich die Grenzlinie zwischen Texas und Mexiko und der Status des 1845 in die Union aufgenommenen Staates Texas geklärt werde. Einige Monate später führte Oberst Kearny seine "Armee des Westens" im Siegeszug in die Plaza von Santa Fe.

Änderungen kamen schnell: eine english-spanische Zeitung informierte die Bevölkerung über die Vorkommnisse in Washington und New York, ein regelmässiger Postdienst verband Missouri mit dem neuen Gebiet, und einmal im Monat durchquerte die Postkutsche die Ebene von Kansas. Die Menge der Güter, die über den Santa Fe Trail kamen, vermehrte sich um ein Vielfaches. Ein neuer Erzbischof veranlaßte die Stadtväter, Kranken- und Waisenhäuser zu bauen und Schulen zu eröffnen. Sogar das Aussehen der Stadt veränderte sich. Weiße Gartenzäune, Giebelhäuser, Blumengärten und Stadtverordnungen, die das Campieren der Karawanen und das Schlachten von Tieren auf der Plaza verboten, kamen mit dem Bevölkerungszuzug aus dem Osten.

Die spanische und indianische Bevölkerung fühlte sich allerdings immer mehr bedroht, da die anglo-amerikanischen Behörden und Siedler ihre spanischen und indianischen Landbesitzrechte nicht anerkannten. Indianerangriffe auf Siedler und Aufstände nahmen zu. Als 1880 die erste Lokomotive in Santa Fe einfuhr, verloren die Indianer und Spanish Mexikaner ihren Kampf um ihren Besitz endgültig an landgierige Spekulanten und Viehzüchter.

Am 6. Januar 1912 wurde Neu Mexiko als der 47. Staat in die Vereinigten Staaten aufgenommen.

Während der zwanziger Jahre kamen viele Künstler, angezogen von Neu Mexikos Geschichte und Bräuchen, seiner schönen Landschaft und ungewöhnlichen Farbtönen nach Santa Fe und Taos. Diese Maler und Schriftsteller vermittelten den Amerikanern betörende Bilder und Beschreibungen von dem, was sie in dem bisher unbekannten Südwesten sahen.

Santa Fe gehört heute mit seinen Opernfestspielen, seinen Konzerten, Kunstgalerien, Theater- und Tanzvorführungen und Museen zu den kulturellen Zentren der Vereinigten Staaten.

## Acknowledgments:

My special thanks are due to:

Mrs. Gabriele Lutz
El Rancho de las Golondrinas
Guadalupe Historic Foundation
Kit Carson Historic Museum
Millicent Rogers Museum
Pecos National Monument


Photographs courtesy of:

Gabriele Lutz  pages 1, 4, 5, 10, 11, 16, 20, 21, 22, 24, 25, 41, 47, 49, 50, 55, 60, 64
Museum of New Mexico, page 3; from Photo Archives, pages 8, 30
Museum of Indian Arts and Culture / Laboratory of Anthropology, page 26, photo by Douglas Kahn
New Mexico Economic and Tourism Department, pages 34, 45, 54, photos by Mark  Nohl
The Santa Fe Opera, page 33, photo by Robert Reck
Wheelwright Museum of the American Indian, page 27, photo by Bruce Hucko


Maps courtesy of:

Elisabeth Hoff

Museum of Fine Arts, 107 West Palace Ave., built in 1917, the first building in the Spanish Pueblo Revival style, was modeled after the 1915 New Mexico State Exposition Building at the San Diego Exposition, which helped promote the rich architectural heritage of the Southwest. The Spanish Colonial-style furniture was designed for the museum.

Museum of Fine Arts. Santa Fe and Taos have attracted writers, poets, musicians, photographers and sculptors since the 1880's, however, it was the painters of the 1920's and 30's who were the most influential on the American art scene with their brilliant light and unusual subjects. The "Art in New Mexico: The Early Years" exhibit is on the second floor.

*Red Hills and Pedernal* by Georgia O'Keeffe, painted during one of the artist's early visits to New Mexico in 1936, belongs to the Georgia O'Keeffe collection of the Museum of Fine Arts. From 1949 on, Georgia O'Keeffe spent summer and autumn at Ghost Ranch and spring at her house in Abiquiu. In 1986, Georgia O'Keeffe died in Santa Fe at the age of 98. More of her paintings, drawings and sculptures can be seen at the Georgia O'Keeffe Museum at 217 Johnson Street.

Palace of the Governors, Plaza, has been in continuous use since 1610. The original structure, called "Casas Reales" (Royal Houses), consisted of workrooms, stables, storage rooms, defense towers, a chapel, a garrison and living quarters of the governor. In 1680, during the Pueblo Revolt, about 1,000 Spaniards, their servants and livestok gathered within the Casas Reales. When the Spaniards fled the city, the Indians remodeled the palace into a multistoried pueblo. Today it houses the History Museum.

Indian artists spread their handmade crafts under the "portal" of the Palace of the Governors.

Around the Plaza.

Sena Plaza, Palace Avenue. In the 19th century, this courtyard was the scene of grand Spanish hospitality. The hacienda for the big Sena family hat 33 rooms and a ballroom big enough to hold the legislative assembly when the capitol burned in 1892.

Photo (ca 1868) of the old "parroquia" (parish church) and East San Francisco Street. Between 1869 and 1886, the new cathedral was built around the old parish church, a simple adobe structure started in 1714, parts of which can still be seen in the Chapel of our Lady of the Rosary.

St. Francis Cathedral. The cornerstone of the cathedral was laid in 1869 by Bishop Lamy. The original French plans for the cathedral called for steeples to rise 160 feet from the two towers, they were never built.

Bishop Lamy, arrived in Santa Fe in 1851 at the height of New Mexico's wild frontier period, during which the influence of the catholic church declined. Bishop Lamy energetically brought his flock back into the church, established schools, orphanages and hospitals, and gradually instilled a sense of refinement into Santa Fe life. Willa Cather described Lamy's life in Santa Fe in "Death Comes For The Archbishop."

Details from the Cathedral. The sixteen door panels depict the history of Santa Fe. Here: the flight of Santa Feans with their "Conquistadora to El Paso del Norte" in 1680. This carved stone angel reminds us of French churches. Lamy employed stonecutters from Italy and France, however the stone came from nearby quarries.

La Coquistadora, was carved in Mexico and brought to Santa Fe in 1625. She was originally known as Our Lady of the Assumption but was renamed "La Conquistadora" (Our Lady of the Conquest) after she accompanied the Spanish into exile from 1680 - 1692 and returned with Diego de Vargas when he reconquered the territory.

The Institute of American Indian Arts Museum, at 108 Cathedral Place, is a division of Santa Fe's IAIA, a nationally recognized college for American Indian artists. The museum houses contemporary American Indian artwork including pottery, basketry, beadwork, sculpture and paintings.

13

Loretto Chapel, 219 Old Santa Fe Trail. The Sisters of Loretto who had arrived in Santa Fe at the request of Bishop Lamy had this Gothic chapel built in the 1870s. They operated a school for girls at the site of the present Inn at Loretto.

Legend has it that upon completion of the chapel the sisters discovered that the architect had forgotten to include in his plans a stairway to the choir loft and that a conventional stairway would not fit. The sisters were distressed and prayed to St. Joseph, the patron saint of carpenters, for help. Before long a carpenter appeared and constructed this circular staircase without a center support or nails. When the mysterious carpenter had finished his masterpiece he disappeared without any pay.

Inn at Loretto.

Barrio del Analco is perhaps the oldest residential neighborhood in the nation. The Spanish who lived on the north side of the river decreed that their Indian allies and servants had to reside on the south side. The Indians built their houses upon the ruins of an old pueblo. Noteworthy are the Gregorio Crespin House (132 E. De Vargas, not shown) and the "Oldest House in the USA" (215 E. De Vargas) which is a good example of adobe construction, the walls are made of poured mud.

San Miguel Chapel, Old Santa Fe Trail/East De Vargas. This chapel was originally built around 1610 by Mexican Indian servants who lived on the south bank of the Santa Fe River. San Miguel was heavily damaged during the Pueblo Revolt, and was rebuilt in 1710. The altar screens were painted in Mexico in 1798, the central statue of St. Michael dates from the seventeenth century.

Santuario de Guadalupe, 100 Guadalupe Street. This adobe church was built between 1776 and 1795 near the end of the Camino Real, a colonial trade route connecting Mexico City with the northern provinces. The oil-on canvas Spanish barock altar painting was created in Mexico City in 1783 by Jose de Alzibar. It was brought in pieces on mule back up the Camino Real and assembled here. The Santa Fe Desert Chorale performs in the Santuario.

The Lensic Theater, built in 1931, was considered the finest film and vaudeville palace of its time in the Southwest. In 1941, Warner Brothers hosted a spectacular world premiere of the film *Santa Fe Trail*. For the premiere Errol Flynn, Olivia de Havilland and Ronald Reagan arrived on a special train chartered for the event. The Lensic reopened in 2001 as the Lensic Performing Arts Center.

Canyon Road was established by the Pueblo Indians as a trail over the Sangre de Cristo Mountains to Pecos Pueblo, which was a thriving trade center. The two-mile-long Canyon Road, flanked by galleries and restaurants is a must for any visitor. One of the best streets to see old Santa Fe homes is the Acequia Madre which translates into "mother ditch" because it irrigated the fields south of the chapel of San Miguel.

Cristo Rey Church, Upper Canyon Road, was designed by John Gaw Meem, the premier architect of Santa Fe's Spanish Pueblo Revival style. The church was built in 1940 primarily with labor by parishioners who worked Saturdays for free. It is said to be one of the largest twentieth-century adobe buildings on earth.

The baroque altar sceen (reredos) of Cristo Rey Church was carved of stone around 1760 for the military chapel – demolished long ago – of La Castrense on San Francisco Street. Visitors may enter through the second door on the south portal.

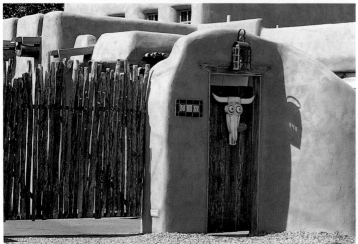
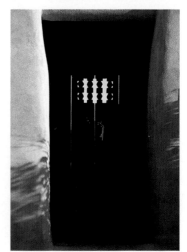

Doors on Camino del Monte Sol.

Museum of Indian Arts & Culture, 710 Camino Lejo. This relatively new museum concentrates on Pueblo, Navajo and Apache Indian peoples of the Southwest. In addition to exhibitions of artifacts from the Laboratory of Anthropology's collection, it presents demonstrations and workshops by Indian basket makers, potters, jewelers and weavers. Shown on this picture is a Zuni jar, ca. 1870, featuring "rainbird" motifs.

Wheelwright Museum, 704 Camino Lejo, was originally built by Mary Cabot Wheelwright to house her extensive records of Navajo ceremonies, myths, songs, sandpaintings, as well as her collection of Navajo basketry, jewelry and textiles. The collection has since expanded to include examples of the craft arts of other Southwestern Indian groups. The museum is in the shape of a traditional Navajo dwelling, the hogan. Shown on this page are Navajo silver and turquoise jewelry pieces.

Above Santa Fe with Sangre de Cristo Mountains (Blood of Christ Mountains) in background.

Caravan on the Santa Fe Trail, 1830. When New Mexico became part of Mexico in 1821, American traders, prohibited by Spanish law to sell their wares in the province, realized they could make fortunes by bringing luxury items from Franklin, MO, to the capital of the New Mexico district. The arrival of the wagon trains from the plains was a spectacle no Santa Fean would have missed, for the "Americanos" also brought news and foreign ideas to the isolated people of the Southwest.

Participants of the annual Mountain Men Rendezvous & Trade Fair ride into Santa Fe. With the opening of the West a new breed of adventurers crossed the plains. These mountain men or fur trappers were intimately acquainted with the vast area stretching from the Missouri River through the Central Rockies and on to the Great Basin beyond. Each summer the trappers convened for a month at a rendezvous to sell their pelts, to resupply and to carouse.

At the rendezvous the mountain men found what they had yearned for all year: company, food, conversation, new clothes, dry shoes, women, gambling, tobacco and booze. A good trapper would come back to the rendezvous with 300 to 400 beaver pelts which he sold for between a thousand and two thousand dollars. Unfortunately, the money seldom lasted through the month of the rendezvous.

The Santa Fe Opera, located on a hilltop north of town, draws world-renowned singers, conductors, directors and designers as well as an international crowd of opera lovers. The founder, John Crosby, envisioned to present each season (July, August) one American or world premiere, one Richard Strauss, one Mozart, one Italian opera and one little-known historic opera.

Fiesta de Santa Fe. The first Fiesta was celebrated in 1712, when it was decreed that De Vargas' reconquest of Santa Fe in 1692 was to be commemorated with an annual fiesta. This celebration blends a mixture of cultures - from De Vargas' "entrada" (historical pageant) to "desfile de las Fiestas" (parade); from the solemn Mass to the burning of "Zozobra" which marks the end of gloom and the beginning of fun.

Indian Dances and Ceremonies. Closest to Santa Fe are the Eight Northern Indian Pueblos stretching from Tesuque to Taos and five Pueblos between Santa Fe and Albuquerque. Each Pueblo has its own pottery style and celebrates its patron saint's day and other ceremonial events with traditional dances, music and feasting. Plan to visit the Pueblos on such days, but call ahead to see if visitors are welcome.

El Rancho de las Golondrinas, La Cienega. The Ranch of the Swallows was a hacienda and the last stopping place for the caravans and travelers on the Camino Real (The Royal Road) from Mexico City. A living museum of the region's Spanish colonial heritage, this working ranch includes 18th and 19th century houses and their outbuildings, a blacksmith shop, several water mills, a winery and vineyards. Also on the grounds are re-creations of a Spanish village, a meeting house and a cemetery.

The main buildings of El Rancho de las Golondrinas were built around a central "placita," with a defensive tower on one side of the fortress-like compound. In case of an attack by hostile Indians the farm animals and wagons were hastily driven into the square and the gates closed.

The Morada de la Conquistadora, El Rancho de las Golondrinas. This meeting house of the Brotherhood of Los Penitentes is a reconstruction of the "morada" at Abiquiu. The Penitentes were a lay brotherhood who devoted themselves to the commemoration of the suffering and death of Jesus Christ and to penitential practices. Their folk religion spread rapidly in Northern New Mexico towards the end of the eighteenth century.

Santuario de Chimayo, Chimayo. This small chapel, which is sometimes called the Lourdes of the Southwest, is one of the most revered places in New Mexico. The ground on which the chapel is built is reputed to have miraculous healing powers. The facade and the religious folk art inside are typical of the Spanish frontier churches of the early nineteenth century. Chimayo is also a center for Spanish weaving.

San Jose de Gracia in Las Trampas (Spanish for "The Traps".) The chapel, built in 1760, is one of the most beautiful Spanish colonial churches in the state. For many years, Las Trampas was the center of the Penitente movement in America. The choir loft of the church is outside so that during processions the singers could be heard. In 1986, Robert Redford filmed *The Milagro Beanfield War* in Las Trampas.

San Francisco de Asis Church in Rancho de Taos was built in 1815 by Franciscans. The mission church was made famous by paintings of Georgia O'Keeffe and the photography of Ansel Adams who called it "one of the great architectural monuments in America". Rancho de Taos was settled by the Spanish in 1716.

Hyde Memorial Park. Hyde Park Road, which ends at the Santa Fe Ski Basin, climbs from seven thousand feet to 10,260 feet.

Several trails start along Hyde Park Road, like the Aspen Vista Trail which leads through aspen, fir and spruce forests to Tesuque Peak (12,040 feet).

Shidoni Foundry, Gallery and Sculpture Garden on Bishop's Lodge Road in Tesuque is a fine art casting facility and show-place. Visitors have the opportunity to watch 2000-degree molten bronze being poured into ceramic shell molds. Works by more than 100 artists are exhibited in the garden and galleries.

Ácoma Pueblo is called *Sky City* for its dramatic location atop a 367-foot-high mesa. Ácoma is believed to be the oldest continuously occupied settlement in the United States; however, of the 465 houses atop the mesa only a few are still lived in. In 1598, Ácoma rebelled against the Spanis forces. In the battle that followed the Spaniards won. As punishment and warning, Governor Oñate ordered that each adult male Ácomese prisoner's foot be cut off.

Pecos National Monument. Ruins of this ancient pueblo go back to the 1400's, when Pecos was a thriving pueblo of 2,000 people. Its quadrangle, built around a central plaza, was four to five stories high, included up to 660 rooms and more than 20 ceremonial kivas. At the time of Coronado's arrival the village was an important trading center between the Plains Indians to the East and the Pueblo Indians to the West. Shown here is a diorama of the North Pueblo displayed in the museum.

Pecos National Monument. The Franciscan friars arrived in the 1600's bringing Christianity, European farming methods, apples, apricots, wheat, cattle and many other things. In return the Indians introduced the Spaniards to their herbal medicine and methods of irrigation, and to such crops as corn, beans and squash. A mission church was erected in 1620 only to be destroyed in the revolt of 1680. The massive walls of the second church served as a landmark to travelers on the Santa Fe Trail.

Chimney Rock at Ghost Ranch. The name Ghost Ranch comes from local Spanish folklore which called it El Rancho de los Brujos - Ranch of the Witches. Today Ghost Ranch is an education and mission center for the Presbyterian Church. Fossil remains of the dinosaur, Coelophysis, which were found at the ranch, can be seen in the Florence Hawley Ellis Museum of Anthropology. Other attractions are a living museum, nature trails and hiking trails.

Madrid, once a thriving coal mining town, was founded in the mid-1800's. It was purchased fifty years later by the Albuquerque and Cerrillos Coal Co. which operated the mines till 1959 when everything was shut down and Madrid became a ghost town. Since then the town has started to come to life again as an artists' colony.

The AT & SF (Atchison, Topeka & Santa Fe Railroad) engine, at the Old Coal Mining Museum in Madrid. In 1880, the first engine steamed into Santa Fe on a spur from the main line which passed through nearby Lamy on its way to Albuquerque. The railroad soon replaced the mule-drawn wagons of the Santa Fe Trail.

Church in Golden. Golden was the site of the first gold rush west of the Mississippi in 1825.

Sandia Crest. The 10,678 feet high summit of the Sandia Mountains offers sweeping views in all directions. Several hiking trails lead through aspen glades and across flowering meadows. The Sandia (Watermelon) Mountains were named because of the pink glow that covers the mountain tops at sunset.

Albuquerque was founded in 1706 in honor of the tenth Duke of Alburquerque (the "r" was subsequently dropped). From the beginning, Albuquerque was a trade and transportation center. The church, San Felipe de Neri, in the center of Old Town, still rests on its thick original walls.

The Albuquerque International Balloon Fiesta features 600 hot air balloons during nine days in October.

Impressions of New Mexico.

Bandelier National Monument, Frijoles Canyon. Inhabited by the Anasazi (the Ancient Ones) more than 600 years ago. They were farming people who grew their squash, beans and corn in the rich soil of the canyon floor and on the mesatops. They built multistoried, apartment-like structures around a central plaza and along the walls of the canyon, and carved dwellings into the porous cliffs.

56

As many as 550 people lived at one time in Frijoles Canyon. Nobody knows for sure why the Anasazi left their cliff dwellings and settled along the Rio Grande, but when the Spanish arrived in the late 1500's the stone rooms in Frijoles Canyon were deserted.

Martinez Hacienda, Ranchitos Road, Taos. This fortress-like hacienda was built around two placitas by Don Antonio Severino Martinez, around 1804. Don Antonio, a trader and owner of caravans in the profitable Chihuahua trade, was also "Alcalde" of Taos. His eldest son, Antonio Jose, became a priest and the spiritual and social leader of the Northern Rio Grande area.

Kit Carson House & Museum, East Kit Carson Road, Taos. Kit Carson came to New Mexico with a caravan commanded by Charles Bent, who later became the first American Governor of New Mexico. In 1843, the famous scout purchased this home as a wedding gift for his bride, Josefa Jamarillo. Three of the rooms are furnished as they might have been when Kit Carson and his family lived there. The museum offers exhibits about Carson and the Mountain Men Period.

Taos Pueblo is the northernmost of the 19 pueblos still in existence in New Mexico. The Tribe is descended from Anasazi Indian culture which flourished in the Four Corners Area of the Southwest from A.D. 100 to A.D. 1200. The Anasazi migration into the Taos area occurred as early as A.D. 900. When Coronado and his men saw Taos in 1540, they believed they had discovered one of the lost cities of gold. Virtually unchanged in appearance the north building has been lived in since about 1450.

Church in Taos Pueblo.

Taos Pueblo. The mountain creek that runs between the North and South Houses flows from sacred Blue Lake, high in the surrounding mountains. In 1970, President Nixon signed the bill returning title of the Blue Lake area to the Pueblo into law, thus ending the Pueblo's 60-year fight for return of its sacred lands, and marking the beginning of a new direction in Indian affairs.

Millicent Rogers Museum, off NM 522, Taos. The museum's original collection consists of southwestern native American jewelry, textiles, baskets, pottery and paintings assembled during the 1940's by Millicent Rogers. In recent years religious and secular artifacts of Hispanic New Mexico have been added, as well as the most extensive collection of Maria Martinez pottery anywhere. The sculpture on this page is by R.C. Gorman, a Navajo artist. It is located in the interior patio of the museum.

Rio Grande Gorge, US 64. A huge split in the earth's crust has resulted in the Rio Grande rift basin which filled with thousands of feet of alluvium from bordering mountains and lava flows from deep within the earth. The Rio Grande Gorge is about 650 feet deep.

# Index Santa Fe

* **Museum of New Mexico** (505-476-6463, www.nmculture.org) oversees four museums in Santa Fe (the Museum of Fine Arts, the Palace of the Governors, the Museum of International Folk Art, the Museum of Indian Arts and Culture) and five historic monuments (Jemez, Coronado, Ft. Sheldon, Ft. Sumner and Lincoln) which are located around the state. The four museums have free admission for ages 16 and under, they are also free for New Mexico seniors on Wednesdays. Passes to the museums and the historic monuments are available.

---

## Santa Fe

**Page** (numbers on maps correspond to page numbers)

1–3    *Museum of Fine Arts, 107 West Palace Avenue, Tel.: 505-476-5072
       Hours: Tues.–Sun. 10–5, Fri. 5–8 (closed Mondays)
       Admission: Yes

       The Georgia O'Keeffe Museum (not shown), 217 Johnson Street, Tel.: 505-946-1000, www.okeeffe-museum.org
       Hours: Mon.–Sun. 10–5, Fri. 5–8 (closed Wednesdays)
       Admission: Yes

4      *Palace of the Governors, The Plaza, 105 W. Palace Avenue, Tel.: 505-476-5100
       Hours: Tues.–Sun. 10–5, Fri. 5–8 (closed Mondays)
       Admission: Yes

9–12   San Francis Cathedral, Cathedral Place, Tel.: 505-982-5619
       Archdiocese of Santa Fe Museum, 223 Cathedral Place, Tel.: 505-983-3811
       Hours: Mon.–Fri. 9–4
       Admission: Donation

13     The Institute of the American Indian Arts Museum (I.A.I.A.), 108 Cathedral Place,
       Tel.: 505-983-8900, www.iaiancad.org
       Hours: Mon.–Sat. 10–5, Sun. 12–5
       Admission: Yes (under 16 free)

**14, 15**    Loretto Chapel, 219 Old Santa Fe Trail, Tel.: 505-982-0092
Hours: Mon.–Sat. 9–6, Sun. 10:30–5
Admission: Donation

**18**    San Miguel Mission, 401 Old Santa Fe Trail, Tel.: 505-983-3974
Hours: Mon.–Sat. 9–5, Sun. 1:30–4
Admission: Free

**19**    Santuario de Guadalupe, 100 Guadalupe Street, Tel.: 505-988-2027
Hours: Mon.–Sat. 9–4
Admission: Donation

**20**    Lensic Theatre, 211 W. San Francisco Street, Tel.: 505-982-0301

**22**    Cristo Rey Church, Upper Canyon Road, Tel.: 505-983-8528
Hours: Daily 7–7
Admission: Free

**26**    *Museum of Indian Arts and Culture, Museum Plaza, 710 Camino Lejo, Tel.: 505-827-6344
Hours: Tues.–Sun. 10–5
Admission: Yes

**27**    Wheelwright Museum of the American Indian, Museum Plaza, 704 Camino Lejo
Tel.: 505-982-4636, www.collectorsguide.com
Hours: Mon.–Sat. 10–5, Sun. 1–5
Admission: Yes

*Museum of International Folk Art (not shown), Museum Plaza, 706 Camino Lejo
Tel.: 505-476-1200, www.state.nm.us/moifa
Hours: Tues.–Sun. 10–5
Admission: Yes

The Santa Fe Children's Museum (not shown), 1050 Old Pecos Trail
Tel.: 505-989-8359, www.sfchildmuseum.org
Hours: Thur.–Sat. 10–5, Sun. 12–5 (during summer also Wed.)
Admission: Yes

Bataan Memorial Military Museum & Library (not shown) 1050 Old Pecos Trail, Tel.: 505-474-1670
Hours: Tue.–Fri. 9–4, Sat. 9–1 (closed Thursdays)
Admission: Free

SITE Santa Fe (not shown), 1606 Paseo de Peralta, Tel.: 505-989-1199, www.sitesantafe.org
Contemporary art, dance, film, art & culture lectures and discussions in an old beer warehouse.
Hours: Wed.–Sun. 10–5, Fri. 10–7 (free tours Sat. & Sun. 2 p.m., Fri. 6 p.m.)
Admission: Yes

Shidoni Gallery, Foundry, Sculpture Garden (shown page 44), Bishop's Lodge Road, Tesuque,
Tel.: 505-988-8001
Hours: Daily (bronze pours every Saturday)
Admission: Free

33     The Santa Fe Opera, P.O.Box 2408, Santa Fe, NM 87504, Tel.: 800-280-4654, www.santafeopera.org

36–38     El Rancho de las Golondrinas, 334 Los Pinos Road, La Cienega, Tel.: 505-471-2261, www.golondrinas.org
Hours: Wed.–Sun. 10–4 from June through September (April, May, October open for guided tours only.) Festivals on
first weekend in June, July, October.
Admission: Yes

## North on the High Road into the Sangre de Cristo Mountains (NM 76, 75 & 518).

39     Santuario de Chimayo, Chimayo, (Easter pilgrimage during Holy Week), Tel.: 505-351-4889
Hours: Daily 9–5:30 (winter 9–4)

40     San Jose de Gracia in Las Trampas
Hours: Daily 11–5 (June–August)

41     San Francisco de Asis Church in Ranchos de Taos, Tel.: 505-758-2754
Hours: Mon.–Sat. 9–5:30 (closed first two weeks every June for renovations)

## Ácoma Pueblo (I-40 W).

45     Ácoma Pueblo Visitors Center, 60 miles west of Albuquerque off I-40,
Tel.: 505-252-1139, 800-747-0181, Sky City Casino 505-552-6017

Hours: Daily 8–5 (last tour is at 4 p.m.). Guided one-hour tours leave in vans from the visitors center, be prepared to walk around unpaved streets.Optional walking trail leads back to center after tour.
Feast Day: September 2; Dances & Celebrations: May 1, June 29, Aug.10, Dec.24-29
Admission: Yes. Fee for photography.

### East to Pecos National Monument (I-25 E, Exit 299).

**46, 47** Pecos National Historical Park, Pecos Pueblo off NM 63, Tel.: 505-757-6414
Hours: Daily 8–6 Memorial Day through Labor Day (after Labor Day 8–5)
Admission: Free

### Northwest to the Rio Chama Valley and O'Keeffe Country (US 84N).

Georgia O'Keeffe Home in Abiquiu (not shown). Tours are on Tuesdays, Thursdays & Fridays. Please call 505-685-4539 well in advance.

**49** Ghost Ranch, Ghost Ranch Road, Tel.: 505-685-4333
Hours: Tues.–Sat. 9–5, Sun. Mon. 1–5 (winter Tues.–Sat. 9–12 & 1–5, Sun. 1–5)
Admission: Donation

### South on the Turquoise Trail to Albuquerque (NM 14).

**50** Madrid has an open house studio/gallery tour along the Turquoise Trail the first Saturday of every month.
Old Coal Mine Museum, Main Street, Madrid, Tel.: 505-438-3780
Hours: Daily 9:30–5:30
Admission: Yes

### West on the Jemez Mountain Trail (NM 502).

Bradbury Science Museum in Los Alamos (not shown), 15th & Central Avenue, Tel.: 505-667-4444
Tells the story of the race to develop the atomic bomb before the Germans, and the scientific discoveries that resulted from the Manhattan Project.
Hours: Tue.–Fri. 9–5, Sat.–Mon. 1–5
Admission: Free

Los Alamos Historical Museum (not shown), 1921 Juniper Street, Tel.: 505-662-6272
Hours: Mon.–Sat. 9:30–4:30, Sun. 11–5
Admission: Free

56, 57    Bandelier National Monument, NM 4, Tel.: 505-672-3861
Hours: Daily from dawn to dusk
Admission: Yes per vehicle

## North to Taos and the Rio Grande (US 84 then NM 68).

58    Martinez Hazienda, 708 Ranchitos Road (NM 522), Tel.: 505-758-1000
Hours: Daily 9–5
Admission: Yes

E.L. Blumenschein Home & Museum (not shown), 222 Ledoux Street, Tel.: 505-758-0505
Home of Taos Society of Artists co-founder.
Hours: Daily 9–5
Admission: Yes

59    Kit Carson Home and Museum, 115 E. Kit Carson Road, Tel.: 505-758-4741
Hours: Daily  9–5
Admission: Yes

Van Vechten-Lineberry Taos Art Museum (not shown), 501 Paseo del Pueblo Norte, Tel.: 505-758-2690
Exhibit of Taos Society of Artists.
Hours: Wed.-Fri.10-5, Sat.1-5, Sun.1-4 (winter: Wed.-Fri.11-4, Sat., Sun.1-4)
Admission: Yes

Fechin Institute Museum (not shown), 227 Paseo del Pueblo Norte, Tel.: 505-758-1710
Home of artist Nicolai Fechin also changing exhibits of other artists.
Hours: Wed.–Sun. 10–2
Admission: Yes

60, 61    Taos Pueblo, off Paseo del Pueblo Norte/US 64, Tel.: 505-758-9593, Taos Mountain Casino 505-758-9430
Hours: Daily 8:30–4:30
Feast Day: September 30; Dances & Ceremonies Jan. 1 & 6, May 3, June 13 & 24 July 25-26, Dec. 24-29
Admission: Yes per vehicle, a fee is charged for cameras.

**53**    Millicent Rogers Museum, NM 522 (4 miles north of Taos), Tel.: 505-758-2462
Hours: Daily  10–5 (November through March closed on Mondays)
Admission: Yes

D.H. Lawrence Ranch and Shrine, NM 522 (not shown, 11 miles). Only shrine is open to the public.

# Calendar of Events

*Santa Fe Convention & Visitors Bureau, 201 W Marcy Street, Santa Fe, NM 87501, 505-984-6760, www.santafe.org;*
*New Mexico Department of Tourism, 491 Old Santa Fe Trail, Santa Fe, NM 87501, 505-827-7400, www.newmexico.org;*
*Museum of New Mexico, P.O.Box 2087, Santa Fe, NM 87504, 505-476-5085, www.nmculture.org;*
*Eight Northern Indian Pueblos, P.O.Box 969, San Juan Pueblo, NM 87566, 800-793-4955; www.IndianPueblos.org*
*El Rancho de las Golondrinas, 505-471-2261, festivals on first weekend in June, July and October; www.golondrinas.org.*

| | |
|---|---|
| January 1–6 | Transfer of Canes Ceremonies in most Pueblos, 800-793-4955 |
| January 6 | Kings Day Celebrations in most Pueblos |
| January 22–23 | San Ildefonso Feast Day, American Indian dances in San Ildefonso Pueblo |
| March/April | Santa Fe Chamber Music Festival, 505-983-2075 |
| April 15 | Corn Dances in Santo Domingo Pueblo, 505-465-2214 |
| May–Nov. | Santa Fe Farmers Market every Tues. & Sat., 7–noon, 520 S Guadalupe Street |
| June 13 | St. Anthony Feast Day, Santa Clara, Taos, San Juan, Picuris Pueblos |
| June 29 | San Pedro Feast Day, Corn Dance at Santa Ana Pueblo |
| July | Annual Eight Northern Pueblos Arts & Crafts Show, Nambe Pueblo, 505-852-4265 |
| | Art Santa Fe International Fair, 505-988-8883, www.artsantafe.net |
| | Traditional & Contemporary Spanish Market Show & Sale, Plaza, 505-983-2640 |
| July–August | Santa Fe Opera, 800-280-4654; Santa Fe Desert Chorale, 800-905-3315; Santa Fe Chamber Music Festival, 505-983-2075 |
| August | Annual Antique Old West & Country Show, 505-992-8929 |
| | Indian Market Art Show, Plaza, 505-983-5220 |
| | Annual Mountain Men Rendezvous & Trade Fair, Palace of the Governors, 505-476-5100 |
| September | Santa Fe Fiesta, Burning of Zozobra, dances, parades, 505-988-7575 |
| | Wine & Chile Fiesta, 505-438-8060 |
| October | Annual Children's Powwow, Wheelwright Museum, 505-982-4636 |
| November | Ski season begins Thanksgiving weekend, 505-982-4489 |
| December | Christmas at the Palace, 505-476-5100 |
| | Las Posadas, outdoor play, Plaza, 505-476-5100 |
| Dec. 24 | Farolitos at the Plaza and at the Cross of the Martyrs; |
| Dec. 24–29 | Dances in most Pueblos, 800-793-4955 |

# BOOKS BY CITIES IN COLOR, INC.

SAVANNAH IN 88 PICTURES
GEORGIA IN 88 PICTURES
COLUMBIA, SC, IN 88 PICTURES
CHARLESTON IN 88 PICTURES
NEW ORLEANS IN 88 PICTURES
ST. AUGUSTINE IN 88 PICTURES
SAN ANTONIO IN 88 PICTURES

RIO DE JANEIRO, BRAZIL
BRASILIA, BRAZIL

VIENNA, AUSTRIA
SALZBURG, AUSTRIA
INNSBRUCK, AUSTRIA

CITIES IN COLOR, INC.
12 BRAEMORE DRIVE, NW
ATLANTA, GA 30328-4845
TEL.: 404-255-1054, FAX: 404-252-7218
E-MAIL: GMHOFF@AOL.COM

WWW.CITIESINCOLOR.COM